Bibliographical Monograph Series No. 7

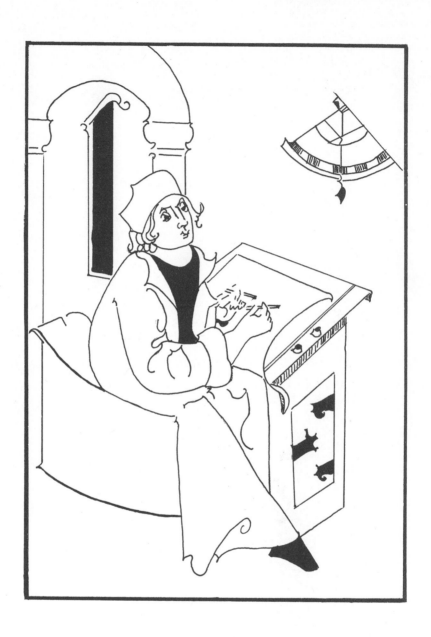

NEO-PHILOBIBLON:

Ruminations on Manuscript Collecting

By JAMES M. OSBORN

Humanities Research Center · University of Texas at Austin

NEO-PHILOBIBLON

$\mathcal{N}EO$-$\hat{P}HILOBIBLON$:

$\mathcal{R}$uminations on Manuscript Collecting

The title of this Feldman Lecture is chosen with some care. The treatise *Philobiblon*, composed in 1345 by Richard Aungerville, bishop of Durham (called Richard "de Bury" after his birthplace, Bury St. Edmunds), describes how he collected his remarkable library and the way it should be cared for. *Philobiblon* is the most popular work on the subject ever written. About forty-five manuscript copies exist, and after its first printing in 1473 at least thirty editions have appeared. Many book lovers have collected these editions. Myriad others have been inspired by this handbook for bibliophiles and have benefited from the common sense and intrinsic interest of the medieval bishop's advice.

Few modern bibliophiles have stopped to realize that Richard de Bury never saw a book in the modern sense, for he died a century before the first book was printed from type in Europe. By "biblon" or "liber" the bishop meant bound manuscripts. He was a fanatic collector of manuscripts because he believed fanatically in the importance of a learned clergy. Thus when the bishop complains of students with dripping noses and black fingernails,[1] who eat fruit and cheese over the open pages, or who scribble in the margins, he is writing of divinity students and ecclesiastical texts. So, too, when he quotes approvingly from Chapter 12 of Ecclesiastes: "Of making many books there is no end," he is urging the transcribing of new copies to multiply the number of texts available.

Today we may consider some of de Bury's methods of col-

[1]*Philobiblon*, chapter 17.

lecting books to have been of questionable morality. He let suppliants know that he preferred to be bribed by gifts of manuscripts instead of gold; so word soon circulated that "one could easier obtain our favor by quartos than by money." The bishop's further statement is charming in its directness:

> Truly, had we loved gold and silver cups, spirited horses, or no small sums of money, we might at that time have stored up a rich treasure for ourselves. But, indeed, we preferred books to pounds, loved parchments more than florins, and cared more for lean pamphlets than fat palfreys.[2]

As a medieval churchman, de Bury believed that the end justified the means when the end was the propagation of divine knowledge.

My own four decades of collecting manuscripts have been active, but can scarcely be called fanatical. Instead of seeking divine knowledge my purpose has been to collect evidence for the use of students working on British literary and historical subjects of the period before 1815. Besides the political changes which occurred at the end of the Napoleonic wars, materials for the study of history also altered greatly as the steel pen replaced the goose-quill, and the steam press revolutionized the printing trade. This terminal date of 1815 has often been exceeded, though I have tried to resist the temptation of the farmer who said, "I am not covetous; I merely wish to own all the land that borders on my acreage." Fortunately this cut-off date has prevented any ambition to compete with the University of Texas Library, world-famous for its riches in nineteenth and twentieth-century English literature. Such ambition would be fruitless, for Mr. Feldman and Texas almost always win. In the pages and generalizations which follow in this "Neo-Philobiblon," I have drawn on my own experiences for examples.

First, a short explanation of the Osborn Collection, which does not have a printed catalogue, and until recently was strictly a private library. The guiding purpose behind the collection was de-

[2]*Philobiblon,* chapter 8.

scribed a dozen years ago by Laurence Witten as "primarily a scholar's accumulation of source materials ... a collection of collections ... for the use of scholars today and tomorrow."[3] He pictured with amusement the way the manuscripts were stashed away in the basement of my home:

> Briefly, the Osborn answer to the housing of all these papers is to save the cartons in which alcoholic beverages are delivered; these cardboard cartons of double thickness and stout construction which once contained a dozen flagons of "Old Forester", "Johnny Walker" or "Gilbey's London Gin" are then filled with manuscripts, each wrapped in paper or other protective covering. Sundry legends have sprung up around this practice, of which the best documented tells of John Crow's delight at finding an Elizabethan manuscript he wished to consult stored in a carton labelled "Old Crow".

A dozen years later, the situation has greatly altered, for the collection is now under professional care, installed as one of the constituent sections of the beautiful Beinecke Rare Book and Manuscript Library at Yale. Here it is being augmented and catalogued, and scholars may consult the manuscripts under ideal working conditions. A large portion of the Osborn Collection already has been given to Yale, as the rest will be in the future. We feel this location has infinite advantages over any attempt to maintain the collection in a building of its own.

In our literary collections, as one would expect, letters and manuscript poetry predominate. More than half of the poetical manuscripts have already been catalogued. Our copies of poems listed in Margaret Crum's *First Line Index to Manuscript Poetry*

[3]In the "Contemporary Collectors" series, *The Book Collector* 8 (1959): 383-396. See also Stephen Parks, "The Osborn Collection: A Biennial Progress Report," *Yale University Library Gazette* 44 (1970): 114-138; and "The Osborn Collection: A Second Biennial Progress Report," *YULG* 46 (1972): 128-152; see also Diane Boito, "Manuscript Music in the James Marshall and Marie-Louise Osborn Collection at Yale," *Notes: the Quarterly Journal of the Music Library Association* 27 (1970): 237-244.

in the Bodleian Library before 1800 have been entered in an inter-leaved set of her volumes. Poems "not in Crum" have been entered on typed cards and filed under first line, attributed au-thor, and title. Already the drawers contain cards for 3,500 poems "not in Crum." Here again we follow the example of the bishop, for despite his clerical purpose in collecting manuscripts, he titled his thirteenth chapter "Why We Have Not Wholly Neglected the Fables of the Poets." In it he proceeded "to show that those who study them [the poets] with due regard are to be held blameless." In de Bury's time all poetry was in manuscript, whereas we have become accustomed to thinking that all good poems have found their way into printed books. Working with manuscripts soon reveals that not all unpublished poems are in-ferior to those which have reached print.

For example, when I was asked to suggest a few Elizabethan poems which might be set to music as part of a celebration planned by the Elizabethan Club at Yale to mark the four-hundredth anniversary of the accession of Queen Elizabeth the First, one of the manuscript poems I selected consisted of five quatorzains, or stanzas of fourteen lines. The text given below is in modern spelling. When reading it, visualize the Elizabethan swain, accompanying his voice with the lute, as he sings of the amorous pain against which he is helpless.

> The Gods of love that sit above,
>   And know me, and know me,
>   How sorrowful I do serve:
> Grant my request that at the least
>   She show me, she show me,
>   Some pity when I deserve.
> That every brawl may turn to bliss,
>   To joy with all that joyful is.
> Do this my dear and bind me
>   For ever and ever your own,
> And as you here do find me,

So let your love be shown:
For till I hear this unity,
   I languish in extremity.

As yet I have a soul to save
  Uprightly, uprightly;
    Though troubled with despair,
I cannot find, to set my mind
  So lightly, so lightly,
    As die before you be there.
But since I must needs you provoke,
  Come slake the thirst, stand by the stroke,
That when my heart is tainted
  The sorrowful sighs may tell
You might have been acquainted
  With one that loved you well:
None have I told the jeopardy
  That none but you can remedy.

Those cursed eyes that were the spies
  To find ye, to find ye.
    Are blubbered now with tears;
And eke the head that Fancy led
  To mind ye, to mind ye,
    Is fraught with deadly fears,
And every part from top to toe
  Compelleth the heart to bleed for woe.
Alas, let pity move you
  Some remedy soon to send me,
And knowing how well to love you,
  Your self vouchsafe to lend me:
I will not boast the victory,
  But yield me to your courtesy.

I read of old what hath been told
  Full truly, full truly,
    Of ladies long ago,
Whose pitiful hearts have played their parts
  As duly, as duly,
    As ever good will could show;
And you therefore that know my case,
  Refuse me not but grant me grace
That I may say and hold me
  To one triumph and truth,
Even as it has been told me,
  So my good lady doth:
So shall you win the victory,
  With honour for your courtesy.

With courtesy now, so bend, so bow,
  To speed me, to speed me,
    As answereth my desire;
As I will be if ever I see
  You need me, you need me,
    As ready when you require;
Unworthy though to come so nigh
  That passing show that feeds mine eye,
Yet shall I die without it,
  If pity be not in you;
But sure I do not doubt it
  Nor anything you can do,
To whom I do commit, and shall,
  My self to work your will, withal.

Probably you hear Shakespeare ringing in your ears. When I
read this poem aloud to my research assistant, Dr. Roger
Lonsdale, now fellow and tutor at Balliol College, Oxford, he
interrupted me to say, "Those lines sound like a song in *Much
Ado*." A step to the bookshelf confirmed the fact: in Act V,

scene ii, the transmuted Benedick voices his lovesickness by
singing these four lines:

> The god of love,
> That sits above,
> And knows me, and knows me,
> How pitiful I deserve.

(Shakespeare's fourth line is a conflation of the third and sixth
lines of the song, perhaps a deliberate misquotation.)

Here then is the only known copy of a poem loved by Shakespeare which for two centuries had eluded his editors. Indeed,
Professor Dover Wilson concluded in the *New Cambridge Shakespeare* that the original is "apparently no longer extant." Scholars
had shown that "The Gods of Love" was one of the favorite
songs of its time, often alluded to and parodied. In 1793 Joseph
Ritson called attention to a "puritanical parody" of it by
William Birch, entitled "The Complaint of a Sinner, Vexed with
Paine." Since Birch's moralized version was entered on the Sta-
tioner's Register in 1562-63 the appearance of the original song
can be given an approximate date. The registers for this period
record several other parodies and answers, all of which attest
to the popularity of "The Gods of Love."

When compared with other poetry of the 1560s this poem is
remarkable for both the quality of its verse and its complicated
structure. The rhyme scheme is unusually intricate for this early
period. Small wonder that the early Elizabethans, accustomed
to the verses of Tusser, Churchyard, and other writers of what
Professor C. S. Lewis has dubbed the "Drab Age," took "The
Gods of Love" to their hearts.

William Birch's parody clinches the identity of the newly found
poem, for Birch employed exactly the same stanza form and,
wherever possible, kept the same rhyme words. Moreover, Birch
stated that the original was written by one "W. E." Ever since
Ritson, scholars have agreed that these initials stand for William
Elderton (d. 1592?), and no other likely candidate has ever been
found.

Elderton is one of the most colorful characters in the Elizabethan pageant. He apparently began life as an actor and in January 1573 directed the Boy Actors of Eton College in a performance before Queen Elizabeth at Hampton Court. He had begun writing poetry before 1559; his "Pangs of Love," one of the most charming songs of the decade, was registered in that year. Elderton soon became the most popular ballad writer of his day, as scores of contemporary references testify. Camden reports that "he did arme himself with Ale . . . when he ballated" and thus Elderton's "ale-crammed nose" (Gabriel Harvey's description) became a stock feature of the tavern literature of the 1580s. Indeed the late Hyder Rollins suggested that Shakespeare may have had Elderton in mind when he created Bardolph of the huge nose. But "The Gods of Love," taken with "The Pangs of Love," shows that Elderton's early powers equalled those of any poet writing in the first years of Elizabeth's reign. He of the ale-crammed nose was a much abler writer than the jibes of his successors have led us to believe.

The recovery of this poem both illuminates a page in Shakespeare and once again illustrates his intimate knowledge of the popular literature of his age.[4] It also shows that many flowers of poesy still blush unseen in manuscript collections.

To return to less poetical matters, most manuscript collections consist of prose documents and letters of literary or historical worthies. Those in our collections have been filed under author, with cross-references to the recipient. At some future date we expect to create a chronological file, so that letters written at the time of a chosen event (e.g. the succession of William III, the death of Queen Anne, or the Gordon Riots) may easily be con-

[4]The manuscript, known as "The Braye Lute Book," was purchased for me at Sotheby's on 23 June 1952 at a relatively modest price by the late Percy J. Dobell, whose learning and judgment have now become legendary. This was one of the few instances in which Mr. Dobell exceeded my authorized bid, an action he justified by writing, "I just couldn't resist it." *Forte fortuna adfuit hic meus amicus.* For further details see *The Times* of London, 17 November 1958, p. 11.

sulted by any interested scholar. Among historical manuscripts, we have made a special collection of parliamentary papers from the time of Queen Mary the First in 1553 until the late eighteenth century. Our diaries for the 1628 Parliament are being used by the Yale Parliamentary Diaries Project. Among our parliamentary collections are the Stanford Papers, preserved by John Brown, clerk of Parliament for two decades after the Restoration.

The "constellation principle" has been behind the acquisition of many manuscripts which at first glance seemed unrelated. Just as a constellation is greater than the sum of its parts, so a gathering of related material supplements and illuminates parts which seem unrelated. (In the physical sciences this is called the principle of synergism.) For example, when David Garrick's biographer, George Kahrl, was collecting information about Garrick's library, he went systematically through our holdings of the papers of eighteenth-century scholars. In a batch of letters from Edward Capell, the early Shakespearean editor, a collection which the British Museum could not match in number and content, Kahrl found welcome information on his subject.

Collecting evidence differs from ordinary autograph collecting, where emphasis is on signatures or specimens of handwriting, though letters with content-value sometimes turn up in autograph collections. Usually autographs are gathered more as relics than for any biographical or scholarly purpose. Among autograph seekers cults seem to thrive. The vandals among them are those who cut signatures out of letters or from fly leaves of books: they deserve to have their ears clipped with their own scissors. One nineteenth-century cult, the Grangerizers who bound or pasted letters in books, were less barbaric, for usually the document remains intact and can be removed for proper preservation.

Of course books are collected for many useful purposes, such as bibliographical variations, though only unique copies or books with annotations can be considered to offer the kind of evidential value possessed by manuscripts. In this matter they differ from

15

mere "association books," volumes which belonged to a famous person or were formerly in a famous library. For example, a copy of the 1640 folio of Ben Jonson's *Works* attracted me because the margins are crowded with the scribblings of Charles Stanhope, second Baron Stanhope (1595-1675), marginalia scrawled mostly while he was in his cups. Besides quotations from Shakespeare, Raleigh, Webster Chapman, and other authors, there are jottings which show Lord Stanhope's personal acquaintance with Ben Jonson and John Donne. One passage reads, "I kneaw Ben Jhonson at Lyons hee trauelld wth yoonge Walt Wrawleigh." This expedition took place in 1613, as Jonson told William Drummond of Hawthornden (first published 1717). On a later page Stanhope wrote:

> You use your feet so well sayd Bacon to Ben Jhonson that I would neeuer haue you use it in anything else.

This incident also occurs in Jonson's *Conversations with Drummond:*

> at his hither comming Sr Francis Bacon said to him, he loved not to sie poesy goe on other feet y^n poetical dactyl and spondae.

These notations on Jonson and other contemporaries contribute enough evidence to ensure that the eccentric and bibulous Lord Stanhope will be remembered long after many saner and soberer peers are forgotten.[5]

Authors' annotated copies of their own books often offer unique evidence, occasionally even new passages or poems. A few years ago the catalogue of a California dealer described a copy of Sir John Denham's 1668 *Poems and Translations* containing, it said, "14 pages of the author's manuscript verses." I asked him to send it on approval. Remembering that the then authoritative modern edition of Denham had stated "no personal letters or manuscripts remain," I inquired on what evidence the bookseller

[5]For other details see "Ben Jonson and the Eccentric Lord Stanhope," *The Times Literary Supplement*, 4 January 1952, p. 16.

had concluded that the new verses were indeed in Denham's hand. He replied that he had been assured by the elderly gentleman from whom he had purchased the volume in England that the verses were in the poet's autograph. While waiting for the book to arrive I felt consoled by the thought that it had been ordered on approval.

Once the volume came I went to work to learn if any Denham scholar had yet succeeded in finding samples of Denham's hand. To my joy some letters had recently turned up in the Public Record Office, and comparison showed the dealer to be correct: the annotations were indeed in Denham's handwriting. Among the poems on the endpapers, three proved to be completely new. All three are satires on Denham's favorite whipping-boy, Sir William Davenant, the poet laureate whose aspirations seemed ridiculous to the wits of Charles the Second's court.

A passage of greater interest occurs in the margin of Denham's most famous poem, *Cooper's Hill.* Here, Denham wrote six new lines to be inserted into the invocation to the River Thames. The poet had been describing the port of London and the ships which brought the wealth of the world up the river to the heart of the city. He inserted the new verses:

> Rome only conquerd halfe ye world, but trade
> One coṁonwealth of th[at] and her hath made
> And though the suñ his beame extends to all
> Yet to his neighbour sheds most liberall
> Least God and Nature partiall should appeare
> Coṁerse makes everything grow everywhere

Then follow the four verses celebrated by generations of poets from Dryden onwards:

> O could I flow like thee, and make thy stream
> My great example, as it is my theme!
> Though deep, yet clear, though gentle, yet not dull,
> Strong without rage, without ore-flowing full.[6]

[6]For texts of the new poems, see "New Poems by Sir John Denham," *The Times Literary Supplement,* 1 September 1966, p. 788.

Other annotated books contain evidential value of the most varied kinds. Many "association" copies have jottings of interest, especially those of eighteenth-century worthies such as the great scholar-collector Edmond Malone, who bought his books not to look at, but to *use*. Malone wrote in the margins and endpapers information of such value that his books have been eagerly acquired by the Bodleian, the British Museum, the Folger Shakespeare Library, and other great repositories of learning.[7] George Steevens, Joseph Ritson, Octavius Gilchrist, Halliwell-Phillipps, and Thorn-Drury are others who turned the endpapers and margins of their books into repositories of learned information. (Parenthetically, the only time I made an unlimited bid at Sotheby's was for a set of books annotated by Thorn-Drury.) Isaac Reed pasted newspaper clippings in his books and added his own neatly-penned comments. His copy of Joseph Spence's *Full and Authentic Account of Stephen Duck* (1731) is a prize item of this kind.

Evidential value of a different kind distinguishes the books of the omnivorous collector Narcissus Luttrell. From 1679 until his death in 1732 Luttrell avidly bought books, pamphlets, poems, and broadsides, many of which are the only copies known to exist. Luttrell's habit of jotting on the title page the price and date of publication has produced a body of invaluable information. I have gathered this data into a chronological list which already contains information on over 4000 items. Besides price and date, Luttrell often made comments on identifications in the text and gave the name of the author. For instance, in his copy of Dryden's *MacFlecknoe*, now at Yale, Luttrell noted Dryden to be the author and added "Ag^t Mr. Thomas Shadwell A good poem." On Shadwell's response, *The Medal of John Bayes*, now in the Dyce Collection, he penned, "By Thomas Shadwell. Ag^t Mr. Dryden. Very severe."[8] Scholars from Malone in the eighteenth

[7]See my article "Edmond Malone: Scholar-Collector," *The Library*, 5th ser., 19 (1964): 11-37.

[8]For evidence that the dates are intended to record the day of publication see "Reflections on Narcissus Luttrell," *The Book Collector* 6 (1957): 3-15.

century to Macdonald in the twentieth have cited Luttrell as their authority for essential facts about books published over a span of fifty years.

So much for some kinds of printed books appropriate in a collection of evidence; let us return to handwritten books and documents. Manuscripts come in all shapes and sizes, so that making generalizations about them is as difficult as arranging and housing them systematically at first appears to be. Bound volumes can be shelved, while single letters and documents are best placed in folders and files. For some categories, such as poems on loose sheets, folders within labeled boxes serve well. Such shelves, files, and boxes lack eye-appeal, in contrast, for example, to the handsome libraries of those who collect bindings. Evidence is an inner value unrelated to aesthetics.

Some generalizations are possible, however, about the collecting of manuscripts. As the first, we may cite the bishop's *Philobiblon,* where he wrote,

> no high price should hinder a man from buying books, if he has the amount asked for them, except when he resists the avarice of the seller, or awaits a more convenient time for buying.[9]

This injunction applies more to manuscript material than to printed books, for every manuscript is unique, even when other copies exist. Most printed items will turn up in other available copies, if the collector has patience and is not intent on some special feature such as "condition" or "association" value.[10] Prices are relative to the values defined by the collector. If a genuine letter in Shakespeare's hand were to be offered at an auction, the price would make history. (Soaring prices of old masters

[9]*Philobiblon,* chapter 3.

[10]Exceptions abound, such as rare early books considered unique, or when all other copies are in permanent repositories, e.g. the quarto of Shakespeare's *King Lear* owned by Kraus in 1971.

19

and French Impressionist paintings already numb our financial senses.) In contrast, seventeenth-century copies of Sir Robert Naunton's account of Queen Elizabeth's court, *Fragmenta Regalia,* are sufficiently numerous to appear for sale nearly every year. The most frequent complaint of collectors is "I could have bought it, but the price seemed too high."

Several great collections have grown up on anticipated income. Sir Thomas Phillipps, perhaps the greatest manuscript and book collector of all time, housed many of his treasures on the Continent to keep them out of the hands of his creditors. A church organist in Chicago, W. N. H. Harding, built up an internationally famous collection of song-books by arranging a modest credit line with the learned bookseller Percy J. Dobell, which he reduced regularly from his salary, without hampering Mr. Dobell from ferreting out desirable new items. At least one great university library in America has anticipated income in order to buy important books and manuscripts at the moment when they become available, a wise action for which scholars today and tomorrow should be eternally grateful.

While endorsing the bishop's admonition in the *Philobiblon* to exorcise the bogey of high price, I concurrently urge rejecting the seductive lures of speculation: the temptation to buy books or manuscripts with the expectation of selling them again at a profit. Cleverer people than we make a business of doing so: these are the professional dealers, and not all of them are financially successful. The collector who buys for resale crosses the line between being a book lover and a bookseller. This is not to deny that dealers may love the objects which pass through their hands, just as wine merchants may relish the contents of their shelves and bins. Speculation corrupts the spirit of a collector, a change in character recognized by his colleagues, whose respect he values most. Auctioneers naturally wish to encourage the idea that the art, book, and manuscript lots they sell are certain to rise in value. Charts of rising prices issued by Sotheby's of London, formerly published in *The Times,* have bolstered this concept. But buyers

20

should realize what stock market patrons have learned, that while the average may go up, the price of individual holdings may lag or shrink. The paths of collecting are lined with the bones of speculators who thought they could predict the vagaries of fashion and outwit the professionals. When you feel enticed to buy for cash profit, remember the "bargains" at the Jerome Kern Library sale of 1929 and the drop in prices of English paintings during the 1930s.

A positive policy my experience leads me to endorse is to buy large lots or collections when opportunity offers. Most of the great American research libraries have been built on this principle. It is sufficient to mention the Huntington, which purchased the Hastings-Huntington manuscripts, the Church, Morschauser, Brown and other book collections; the Folger, where the Harmsworth library looms so large; and the University of Texas at Austin, with the Aitken and Wrenn collections. (The recent purchase of the Silver collection by the Newberry Library, though it has left ruffled feathers elsewhere, is an example of applying this principle.) Yale and Harvard each missed the greatest opportunity of this millennium when they declined the chance to buy the submerged bulk of the Phillipps collection for a mere $750,000, only one-twentieth of the sum since realized from the portions already sold.

In building the Osborn Collection we have found the application of this principle consistently rewarding. My first large lot was the papers of Joseph Spence, sold by the Duke of Newcastle at Sotheby's in February 1938. His Grace stipulated that the twenty-two lots, some of them large boxes full of correspondence, fugitive poems, and other documents, should be offered together against a reserve price. Then only a graduate student at Oxford but already a budding collector of manuscripts, I became the final bidder. My two thick volumes of Spence's *Observations, Anecdotes, and Characters of Books and Men* have been the most obvious fruit of this purchase.[11]

[11] Some by-products are "The First History of English Poetry," in *Pope and His Contemporaries,* edited by James L. Clifford and Louis A. Landa

Among other large collections we have kept together, a few may be mentioned. Sir Charles Blagden (1748-1820), longtime secretary of the Royal Society, whom Dr. Johnson praised both as a "delightful fellow" and for his "copiousness and precision of communication"[12] left boxes of correspondence, papers on scientific subjects, and diaries. At first the diaries seem to offer little but detailed accounts of the weather. Later volumes record his visit to America during the Revolutionary War, with pages reporting incidents such as the criticism by British officers of General Howe after the Battle of Brandywine. Similarly, unnoticed by the dealer, among these Blagden papers was a letter from Benjamin Franklin. We also found a batch of papers which came from Blagden's ancestor, Sir Matthew Hale (1609-1676). Among them is a draft of the agreement between the executors of John Selden (including Hale) and the curators of the Bodleian for transfer of Selden's library to the Bodleian for which the "Selden End" was built.

During the past year a large group of seventeenth-century papers which we purchased at Sotheby's produced a discovery which the *New York Times* featured across the front of the

------

(Oxford: Clarendon Press, 1949), pp. 230-250; "Pope, The Byzantine Empress, and Walpole's Whore," *Review of English Studies,* new ser., 6 (1955): 372-382; " 'That on Whiston' by John Gay," in *Papers of the Bibliographical Society of America* 56 (1962): 73-78; "Addison's Tavern Companion and Pope's 'Umbra', " in *Philological Quarterly* 42 (1963): 217-225; "Spence, Natural Genius and Pope," in *Philological Quarterly* 45 (1966): 123-144; "Swiftiana in the Osborn Collection at Yale," in the *Dublin University Review* 4 (1967): 77-83; "Joseph Spence's 'Collections Relating to The Lives of the Poets'," in *Harvard Library Bulletin* 16 (1968): 129-138; and Appendixes H and I in Maynard Mack's edition of Pope's *Iliad and Odyssey* in *The Poems of Alexander Pope* (London: Methuen & Co., 1969), vol. vii, pp. 594-606.

[12]*Boswell's Life of Johnson*, edited by George Birkbeck Hill, rev. and enl. ed. by L. F. Powell (Oxford: Clarendon Press, 1934-1950), vol. iv, p. 30.

second section (15 May 1971, p. 33).[13] These were the papers of the diplomat Theobald Taaffe (d. 1677), Earl of Carlingford. We bought them because of several constituent correspondences, especially letters written to Taaffe by Sir William Temple. In cataloguing the Carlingford papers we were puzzled by a series of two dozen letters signed only with a cypher. Written from Brussels and other places on the Continent in the 1650s, they turned out to be in the hand of King Charles II. These new letters contribute significantly to knowledge of the Merry Monarch's youthful activities before his restoration to the throne in 1660, including some of the young ladies he favored.

Manuscripts of "the Great Doctor Burney" and his family are another treasure trove in the Osborn Collection. To the original nucleus other groups have been added, including the collection of Percy Scholes, one of Burney's biographers. Soon after acquiring the first nucleus we were able to buy a dealer's entire catalogue of Burney papers before it was mailed out to the public. (This dealer's inexperience permitted him to list under "Ebor, William," a letter from William Markham, archbishop of York! Even Macaulay's schoolboy would know that "Ebor" is the abbreviation of the Latin name for York, as "Cantuar" is for Canterbury.) Recently we repeated this procedure by acquiring a collection of letters and documents relating to agreements between authors, publishers, and booksellers which a dealer had gathered for a special catalogue. The advantages of buying a whole catalogue are considerable, for in return the dealer is usually willing to accept a large discount, because he saves the cost and effort of replying to hundreds of letters. His capital can then be reinvested in new stock.

Here it may be appropriate to mention one great collection we acquired over a decade ago but gave to the Bodleian because that is the appropriate home for it. The entire literary remains of the

[13]Based on Stephen Parks and Timothy Crist, "Undiscovered Letters of Charles II," *The Times Literary Supplement*, 30 April 1971, pp. 507-8, reprinted in *Yale University Library Gazette* 46 (1971): 97-108.

Oxford novelist Joyce Cary, including his books, manuscript drafts, correspondence, and other papers filling over a hundred boxes are now kept together in the Bodleian. Several recent books on Cary testify to the value and variety of the Cary archive.

Once a collector or library has acquired a special collection, it is wise to "build to strength" when possible, instead of pursuing tangential items. Occasionally a new archive of material will suddenly appear in the sales room and pose for the collector a dilemma or series of dilemmas. For example, a mass of Richard Brinsley Sheridan papers owned by one of his descendants has recently gone under the hammer at Sotheby's offered in twenty-eight lots which realized a total of almost £11,000. Our bids, all unsuccessful, were concentrated on correspondence not printed in Cecil Price's edition of *Sheridan's Letters*. We attempted to invest in them, leaving the other lots, particularly the theater materials, for collections specializing in such subject matter. Unless the collector attempts to build to strength, he will soon extend himself as far as the farmer mentioned earlier, who coveted all land bordering on his own.

Often private information can lead to notable acquisitions. Robert Super, the biographer of Walter Savage Landor, learned that I had bought the seventeen letters from Robert Browning to Landor's niece. They describe in vivid detail the living arrangements Browning had set up for the aged poet who had been turned out, like King Lear, by his suffering family. Super got in touch with the Landor heirs, a step which resulted in the purchase of the remaining family correspondence. To cite another instance, the late John Hayward a few months before his death called my attention to the catalogue description of a seventeenth-century manuscript of poetical and prose meditations which had struck his eye. He had thoughtfully telephoned a Birmingham bookseller to reserve it for me. After the manuscript reached New Haven, study confirmed what I had suspected, that it is an unknown volume of *Select Meditations* in the autograph of the seventeenth-century poet and mystic, Thomas Traherne.[14]

[14]"A New Traherne Manuscript," *The Times Literary Supplement,* 8 October 1964, p. 928.

Examples abound in other areas: the music critic Jack Diether, knowing my wife's admiration for Gustav Mahler, told us about a major Mahler work still unpublished. This led to correspondence with the composer's nephew and ended with the acquisition of Mahler's glorious *Das Klagende Lied.* Now recorded,[15] the manuscript produced half an hour of hitherto unavailable Mahler for full orchestra, chorus, and soloists. At the suggestion of another music critic, the widow of a German musician telephoned to offer us a letter of Jacques Offenbach. While declining it politely, we learned she had correspondence from several eminent contemporary musicians, and we ended by buying a batch of early letters from Paul Hindemith.

Thomas W. Copeland, editor of the monumental *Correspondence of Edmund Burke,* has over many years helped us build the largest Burke holdings in America. Cecil Price has performed similar "bird dog" service in calling to our attention the letters of Richard Brinsley Sheridan and Lord Chesterfield.

Special mention should be made of the kindness shown by the librarian of another university, Wyman Parker of Wesleyan at Middletown, Connecticut. He had purchased for his institution a large collection of the books and papers of William Force Stead (1884-1967), a close friend from my Oxford days. Stead was a minor poet himself, but the intimate of great poets. After his death we acquired from his family a large quantity of Stead's correspondence and literary papers. Unknown to the family, a packing case of further correspondence had been misplaced in storage and somehow came into the hands of a dealer who sold them to Wesleyan. Parker had seen references to me in Stead's papers and called his purchase to my attention. Once Parker saw the main corpus of Stead manuscripts on our shelves he said, "They ought to be together," and released them for the price he had paid.

Among the combined Stead papers three dozen letters from

[15]Columbia M2-30061, by the London Symphony Orchestra under Pierre Boulez.

T. S. Eliot in the decade 1927-1938 are of special interest. They provide details of Eliot's decision to become an Anglican, his baptism by Stead, then chaplain of Worcester College, Oxford, and his confirmation in the Church of England, arranged by Stead. Other notable correspondences include twenty-one letters from William Bulter Yeats and more than sixty from Edmund Blunden. Recently we learned that the other side of this correspondence with Blunden had come to the University of Texas Library, our penalty for daring to venture into the twentieth century, where Texas is so eminent. We have now exchanged copies of the letters, so the full Blunden-Stead correspondence is in both institutions.

For the collector of manuscript evidence such as we have been discussing the chief source of supply obviously is the professional dealers. Bishop de Bury described the situation in the fourteenth century. He reported in his *Philobiblon:*

> Besides all these opportunities set forth above, we obtained the notice of stationers and booksellers not only within the bounds of our native land but throughout the kingdoms of France and Germany and Italy, for our money flew before us. Nor did any distance stop them, nor any storm at sea deter them, nor did money fail them for the charges, that they should not send or bring to us the books of our desire. They knew full well that their hope resting in our bosom could not fail them and that there was to be had of us full repayment with interest.[16]

As investors who take risks, dealers are entitled to a fair profit. For their knowledge and professional experience they deserve the reward of their endeavors. The function of bringing the collector together with objects of real or potential interest is a valued service. It is a fact of business life that most dealers in books and manuscripts do not make fortunes: like farmers they have chosen a way of life for rewards other than great riches. It is a way of making a living while enjoying other pleasures. Actually, dealing

[16]*Philobiblon*, chapter 8.

in books and manuscripts does not pay well enough to attract adequate recruits to the business Like other collectors I have benefited from the friendship of numerous dealers while simultaneously profiting from their knowledge. Each of us has gained from our congenial relationship. The results of such mutual trust and understanding are manifest in many great institutional libraries.

As this paper should have made clear by now, I believe that the highest satisfaction in collecting comes to those who are not content merely in *having*, or merely in building up a mass of evidence. The greatest pleasure, I am convinced, is achieved by those who can combine having with *being*, pleasure derived from turning the collection to useful purposes. I point to the examples of Edmond Malone, Francis Douce, and others who based their scholarly writings on their own collections. In our own time Wilmarth Lewis has done the same with the *Correspondence of Horace Walpole*, as has Sir Geoffrey Keynes with John Donne and William Blake. Others could be named whose collections are, and will continue to be, the source of literary and historical knowledge. To borrow a word from Isaac Walton, these are "The Compleat Collectors" to whom landing a catch is not enough; they angle for fish which will nourish knowledge.

*The Humanities Research Center in Austin issues eight hundred
copies of this book which is set in Press Roman on the IBM
Selectric Composer. The title page is hand-set Cancellersca Bastarda
designed by Jan van Krimpen. The paper is sixty-five pound Adena Text
and the binding cloth is G. S. B. Bookcloth, Style five hundred thirty-five.
The illustrations were drawn by Terry Galloway from woodcuts in
Achatius Morbach's "Dialogus festivus in quo medicaster . . . "
published by F. Paypus in Nuremberg in the early sixteenth century.*

Design and typography by William R. Holman, March 1973.